What Is Hotter Than The Fire?

Danny Phiri

AUSTRALIA

Danny Phiri C/- Intertype
Unit 45, 125 Highbury Road
BURWOOD VIC 3125
www.intertype.com.au

Ordering Information:
Quantity sales. Special discounts are available on quantity purchases by corporations, associations, and others. For details, contact the "Special Sales Department" at the address above.

What Is Hotter Than Fire? / Danny Phiri —1st ed.
ISBN 978-0-6452042-0-9

Contents

i

This book is dedicated to my grandchildren.

The book draws its title from a Proverb: "When you see a Rat run into the Fire, then know that what it is running away from is hotter than the Fire."

=

Preface

What is hotter than the fire? The author tries to explore this question in the context of social aspects of life. Almost every living organism avoids the fire, but for it to run straight into the fire may indicate that the fire is less hot and can be used as a refuge.

The author also looks at other proverbs and explores their significance in the lives of many young people, including adults, as used in the Zambian context. The use of animal stories adds the beauty of nature that Zambian families, especially in the villages, are closely linked to.

I cannot compare this book to any other on this subject matter in that it is unique. I would encourage you to take the 'journey' with the author as per his invitation.

Gertrude G. Phiri

Introduction

Dear reader, thank you for coming along with me on this journey of trying to explain the meanings of the Zambian proverbs to our children and young people. A proverb or a 'wise saying', is defined by Online Oxford Dictionary as *a short, well-known pithy saying, stating a general truth or piece of advice. A proverb (from Latin: proverbium) is a simple concrete, traditional saying that expresses a perceived truth based on common sense or experience. They are often metaphorical and use formulaic language. Collectively, they form a genre or folklore. However, almost every culture has its own unique proverbs."* It is therefore important, for you the reader, to understand that these proverbs may be unique to a Zambian context.

In Zambia, the proverbs are usually used to summarize a long story, and shortens the time required to narrate the details. The proverbs are used to hide the actual meaning of what is being talked about so that those who do not know the context in which the proverb was formulated would not understand what is being said. Proverbs are also used to provide advice or teaching to young people. In rare cases, the proverbs are used to urge the listener to make their own conclusion or formulate their own meanings of what is being said.

In view of the importance of proverbs to either advise or educate our young people, I have found it necessary to put on paper what I learnt from my parents, other elders in Zambia and elsewhere for the sake of my two grandchildren, Micah Zakhele Tshabalala and Khalif Danny Phiri, and others who are yet to come after them, for them to understand some of these proverbs. This, I hope will prepare them enough to adequately communicate with their extended family members in Zambia, and elsewhere in the world. Just like my parents, and other adults in my community, did to make it easier for me to understand the context of each proverb, I have also used the stories for my children and grandchildren to understand the proverbs. Some proverbs can be explained using many different stories, but I have chosen to use only those stories that I still remember very well.

Most of the stories in Zambian context are around the animals, usually considered to have been able to talk to each other, in some cases even with human beings. The setup is in the pre-industrial times, where electricity, modern communication gadgets and civilization had not yet been achieved. I also want you the reader to understand that in Zambia, Rabbit the Hare, is commonly and popularly known as Kalulu. Kalulu is known to be a trick-star, subtle and usually a liar. If someone is described as Kalulu, then most people are usually careful in accepting anything said by them. On the other hand, a person described as a Hyena, is considered to be silly, dull, greed and unkind. Most people do their best to avoid associating with such a person.

Dilemma:

Although the stories are easier to tell in the local languages, it is challenging to fully pass on the same emphasis and meanings into another. In many instances the sentence may be longer in English than in local language, such as in Chichewa, although the meaning and wisdom behind the proverb does not change. An example of a proverb in Chichewa would be: "*Safunsa anadya phula*", while in English it reads as "*A person who does not ask ended up eating bee-wax*"; three words in Chichewa and more than eight in English.

In the Bible there is a book specifically dedicated to proverbs by King Solomon. As expected, some proverbs are more straight forward and easy to understand while others are not. It is true to say that once someone explains the context, most people begin to enjoy proverbs and frequently use some of them in their day-to-day speeches; something I hope you the reader, my children and grandchildren will do.

With the above introduction, I think we are ready to take a dive into some of them and their stories for us to understand.

Hotter Than The Fire

WHEN YOU SEE A RAT RUNNING INTO THE FIRE,
THEN KNOW THAT WHAT IT IS RUNNING AWAY FROM
IS HOTTER THAN THE FIRE

This proverb makes the listener wonder what could be hotter than the fire. The proverb is used when people cannot find the reason or cause of the event. Just as it is not easy to find what could be hotter than the fire, the proverb does make the listener realise that the matter being discussed or being dealt with has no easy answer. Therefore, many adults use the proverb to help children understand that elders will not provide an answer to everything, and they will also not openly say they do not know the solution.

To help children and young people understand this proverb, one of the stories told include the one below:

In a certain village, lived a very intelligent little boy. They named him Nthambi, meaning branch, because he was not like the other children. The parents recognized his unique intelligence from a tender age. Nthambi was able to solve complex puzzles and provide answers to very complex questions for his age. His parents were excited about their child and sought all the necessary support to have Nthambi's unique talent developed fully. His parents would follow any lead that pointed to getting any assistance to put Nthambi in a better school.

After many attempts, his parents heard of a prominent businessman who everyone said was very kind and supportive. Nthambi's parents approached the businessman to try their luck. The businessman agreed to have a chat with both the parents and Nthambi. The businessman was impressed after talking to him and offered to sponsor Nthambi. The Businessman also offered to look after Nthambi in his own house. The parents were happy as they did not have means to meet the boy's needs.

Nthambi progressed very well in school and was placed in the class of the talented children. He graduated with distinctions in all the courses and was the best engineering student. Nthambi was sought after by many companies. He had a very difficult time deciding which company to join. He finally chose to join a company that offered him excellent conditions which included free accommodation, various fringe benefits as well as three international flights a year anywhere in the world for holidays. Many of Nthambi's relatives and friends envied him.

The businessman that helped educate and raise him, told Nthambi and his parents, that he did not expect anything from either Nthambi or the parents for the work he had done in supporting

Nthambi. He was happy that Nthambi was contributing to the wellbeing of both the community and his own family. He wished Nthambi well in his career and life.

Nthambi worked very hard and received many awards and recognitions. He set very high standards in whatever he did. All his friends and people that knew Nthambi acknowledged that he was truly a uniquely talented person. Nthambi did not use his prestigious career or performance to boast or look down on people. He was humble and well cultured.

After working for some years and having settled, Nthambi went to his parents and asked them to help him find a wife. This pleased his parents and all his friends. A very beautiful girl was found, and a very big wedding feast was held. The businessman was the Guest of Honour. In his speech the businessman praised the family for their commitment in seeing Nthambi become what he was. After the wedding, Nthambi took his wife and returned to the City where he continued with his work.

After few years, something happened that changed Nthambi's life. One day Nthambi woke up and told his wife and family that he was quitting his job without any notice. Nthambi also refused to leave the house; he remained in the bedroom and did not want to see anyone that came to the house. Nthambi did not even want to meet his Company's representatives that came to find out what was happening with him as he had not been to work for many days.

Nthambi's wife, parents and friends became worried. They did not understand what had happened to Nthambi that changed his life. As many people asked questions and could not find the answers, others started speaking using the proverb in order to avoid saying things that children could misinterpret; they said; *'when you see the rat running into the fire then know that it is running away from something hotter than the fire'*. No one could explain what happened to Nthambi until his death.

Trees Get Slippery

THE DAY THE MONKEY IS DESTINED TO DIE, ALL THE
TREES GET SLIPPERY

This proverb is used to educate young people to be on a lookout for strange occurrences or happenings in their lives. The happenings could be a warning to them of impending danger. The belief being that whenever something is to go wrong, such is preceded by several minor incidences.

To assist young people to remember the proverb, adults tell stories like the one below:

There was a very talented young man called Chidabwitso, but everyone called him Chida in short. Although Chida was very talented in performing the traditional dances and singing, he was very humble. Many people liked Chida not only for his humility, but generosity and kindness too. He was always surrounded by both his peers and slightly older boys and girls who enjoyed his singing whenever he was not performing the traditional dances.

Chida used to compose songs that had relevance to the way people lived at the time. Many people loved his songs.

Chida was away from his home and village most of the time due to being hired to perform traditional dances and sing during various functions that included weddings. This continued absence from home started to be a concern for his wife. Chida's wife did not complain knowing that their livelihood depended on what her husband was doing. She decided to be accompanying him wherever he went to perform. This worked well until they had a baby. Chida loved his baby and eventually reduced the number of performances so that he could be home with his wife to help look after the baby.

One day Chida was hired to perform at a place very far from his village. His wife could not travel with Chida as the baby was still too young to be taken on such a long trip. She was happy for her husband to go without her. She prepared food, clothes and the things needed for the performance.

A day before Chida was to leave, his wife told him that she was not comfortable with him going for the function. Chida did not understand why his wife had a sudden change of mind about his going despite preparing things for his trip. Even Chida's wife did not fully understand why she did not want her husband to travel, she told him that she just felt uncomfortable.

Chida left the village as planned. He left with friends who assisted carrying his equipment, food and other things he had packed. Just a few meters from his house, Chida bumped into a stump in the road and almost fell to the ground. He managed to regain his balance after staggering for a few steps. One of his friends told Chida that such happenings at the start of a trip was not a good sign. However, Chida did not think it was necessary to cancel the trip and disappoint those that had hired him and the expected audience. The friend agreed with Chida and they continued on their journey.

After walking for several hours, they came to a river which was nearer to their destination. They drank some water and rested before resuming the trip knowing that they would reach their destination shortly. They had just left the river when suddenly they saw a Lion in front of them. They were gripped with fear and started to scream for help while others scampered in all directions trying to find the nearest tree to climb for safety. The Lion charged at them and went straight for Chida. Chida fell to the ground and the Lion leaped into the air to land on him.

The Lion had all its teeth out and was about to go for Chida's neck when suddenly Chida saw the Lion fall on its side. The Lion had been shot by the hunter who had been tracking it for having attacked his cattle. Although the Lion had been shot in time to stop it killing Chida, it had already mauled his leg, which was not only bleeding but had been broken. Chida had fainted by the time the Lion was lifted off his legs.

The hunter and his friends lifted Chida and took him to the hunter's village where he was treated until he regained his consciousness. With the leg broken, Chida could not continue with his journey. The friends carried him back to the village where his family and wife continued to nurse him.

When the people in his village were told of all that Chida had experienced prior to and on his journey, they said that there were many signs that should have made Chida reconsider his trip. The elders in the village concluded by using the proverb, '*The day the Monkey is destined to die, all the trees get slippery*'.

An Axe In His head

HE WHO DOES NOT ACCEPT ADVISE ONLY REALISED
AN AXE IN HIS HEAD

This proverb is stated in three different ways: 'He who does not ask ended up soaking his food in the water' or 'He who does not accept advise only realized an axe in his head' or 'he who does not ask ate bee-wax'. This proverb aims to encourage young people to willingly accept advice and correction. Young people are also encouraged to seek advice and guidance from others, especially the elders in their community or society. They are cautioned against depending on their own wisdom or knowledge, which may result in them facing difficulties. It warns that a young person may experience trouble or face tough situations if they choose to ignore elders' counsel or guidance.

To explain this proverb to young people, grandparents and elders in a village would tell various stories, and one of those stories that I still remember very well is this one:

Once upon a time when animals could gather in peace and enjoy the socialization together, it is understood that they would also exchange various ideas, among them was the planning for their young ones' marriages. It was during such gatherings that most animals showed off their special talents or skills. Animals would also learn of what has been happenings in their communities as stories were shared. Rabbit the Hare, also known as 'Kalulu', is known to have used these gatherings to show off his skills. Although some animals thought that Kalulu was very wise and intelligent, most knew Kalulu as being very crafty. However, due to his style of narrating things in subtle ways, some believed that Kalulu was very intelligent and wise.

The Elephants would not usually attend these gatherings as they required a lot of space due to their massive sizes. Their inability to attend most of these gatherings meant that elephants missed out on a lot of information and did not know a lot of other animals' behaviors, including Kalulu's craftiness. The only thing Elephants knew from the hear-say was that Kalulu was very intelligent and wise.

One day the daughter of the Chief Elephant fell in love with a Crocodile. As was the case at the time, the marriage had to be normalized by sending the go-in-between to ensure all matters were sorted out before the wedding could take place. The Chief Elephant called for Kalulu and asked him to be the go-in-between as the Chief Elephant believed that Kalulu would be a very good negotiator for the family in making necessary negotiations for his daughter. However, when the Tortoise heard that the Chief Elephant had asked Kalulu to be the negotiator, he was concerned. The Tortoise went to see the Chief Elephant with a view to warning him about the Crocodile's intentions to harm his daughter and about Kalulu being asked to be the marriage negotiator.

When the Tortoise arrived at the Chief Elephant's place, he was welcomed and offered food, as was the culture when welcoming visitors. After the meal, the Chief Elephant asked the Tortoise the reason for his visit. The Tortoise told the Chief Elephant that the Crocodile was not really interested in marrying his daughter but to have her as part of their food, and that Kalulu was a liar and not a good negotiator. He told Chief Elephant that Kalulu was crafty and would not tell the Chief Elephant the truth. Before the Tortoise could provide further details on his allegations, the Chief Elephant got annoyed thinking that Tortoise was just wanting to prevent his daughter getting married to the Crocodile and that Tortoise was being malicious against Kalulu. The Chief Elephant chased the Tortoise away and almost crushed the Tortoise with his foot. He believed Kalulu was a good negotiator for his daughter's marriage. This was because the Chief Elephant did not have much information on Kalulu and did not know that he was crafty. Tortoise managed to avoid being trampled on and quickly went away from the presence of the Chief Elephant.

The relationship between the Chief Elephant's daughter and the Crocodile grew stronger each day. As the Chief Elephant's daughter seemed to be getting more closer to the Crocodile, Crocodile thought that it was time to invite the Chief Elephant's daughter to visit his parents' home near the large pool, where the family lived. The Chief Elephant's daughter was first reluctant as she believed that Crocodile was supposed to first see her father and begin the process of their marriage before expecting her to visit his parents. The Crocodile was in a hurry to have his meat as he would salivate each time he saw the Chief Elephant's daughter and would visualize dragging her into the water and eating her. The Chief Elephant's daughter and her father, the Chief Elephant, did not know that the desire of the Crocodile was not really to marry the daughter but to have her as a meal for the family.

To convince the Chief Elephant's daughter to visit him near his parents' home, Crocodile thought of a plan. He pretended to be sick and sent the message to his fiancé, the Chief Elephant's daughter. When the news reached the Chief Elephant's daughter that Crocodile was unwell but would love to see her, she went and told her father. The Chief Elephant called for Kalulu to seek counsel as to whether it would be alright for his daughter to visit her fiancé at his parents' home. Although Kalulu doubted the Crocodile's sickness and knew that the Chief Elephant's daughter would most likely be in trouble, he decided to hide the truth and instead told the Chief Elephant that Crocodile's family was very good, were respected by most animals and that a visit by his daughter would strengthen his prospects of having a very good negotiation.

The truth is that although most animals suspected the Crocodile family to be very dangerous, they did not have evidence of how cruel the Crocodile family was as there was never an animal that escaped the attack of these Crocodiles. They would usually wait until an animal was alone near the pool before pouncing on it and dragging it into the water. As a result of their skill in killing other animals, there was no one to tell the story of their vicious attacks on animals.

The Chief Elephant agreed to let his daughter visit the fiancé, and a message of her intentions to visit was sent to Crocodile and a date and time suggested. However, Crocodile realized that the suggested time of the midday was not good as that was the time most animals would be at the river drinking water. So, he sent a message to the Chief Elephant's daughter that midday was not suitable as that was the time that he was receiving his medication. He suggested that a suitable time would be just before sunset or early in the morning.

The news of Crocodile's request to have the Chief Elephant's daughter visit him at the pool was leaked to the Tortoise, who, despite having been chased by the Chief Elephant, did not want to see the Chief Elephant's daughter being harmed. As he could not risk his life again by going back to the Chief Elephant, the

Tortoise decided to prove his allegations against the Crocodile by hiding near the pool to see what was going to happen. The Tortoise shared the story with his family and friends and requested that they find time to be near the pool early in the morning and evening, just when the sun was setting. The aim was to quickly alert the Chief Elephant should they see his daughter get into trouble.

A day came when Chief Elephant's daughter was going to visit the Crocodile. She beautified herself with the latest fashion and looked stunning. When she arrived near the pool, where Crocodile was with his family, he could not hold his excitement and eagerness to pounce on the Chief Elephant's daughter. The Chief Elephant's daughter did not suspect anything as she thought that her fiancé was just overjoyed to see her. He was all over her and she had to restrain him. He invited her to draw closer to the pool. The Chief Elephant's daughter noticed that the other family members were opening their mouths and seemed to give signals to the Crocodile to do something. This made her hesitate from drawing closer to the pool. As the sun was setting and that the Chief Elephant's daughter would want to go back, the Crocodile became desperate and needed to act quickly.

The Crocodile sensed that the Chief Elephant's daughter was getting suspicious and could turn around and go further away from the water, he pretended to want to kiss her but instead, bit her nostrils. He started pulling her towards the water. The Chief

Elephant's daughter realized that her life was in danger and started to struggle to free herself. She tried to free herself and pulled with all her mighty while shouting for help. But as it was too late, there were no animals nearby to assist her. She pulled trying to free herself from the Crocodile's teeth, but the Crocodile also pulled not wanting to lose his catch. It was really a struggle that went on for a long time. The Crocodile would pull this way trying to make her lose balance, but the Chief Elephant's daughter also pulled the other way.

The Tortoises hiding near the pool saw this and realized that if they did not act quickly, the Chief Elephant's daughter was going to die. As they were many, they started sending the messages through their line which they had formed with their friends. Within a short time, the message reached the Chief Elephant that his daughter was in danger.

Due to the pulling that was going on, the Chief Elephant's daughter was having her nostril stretching and Crocodile's mouth also stretching. After what seemed like an endless struggle, the Chief Elephant arrived near the pool, with other animals that had wondered why the Chief Elephant was running at a break-neck speed, crushing trees on the way. The animals heard the cry for help as they were drawing near the pool. However, being afraid of the Crocodile's family, they stood at a distance and watched.

The Chief Elephant arrived at the pool and saw that his daughter was being dragged towards the water by the Crocodile, her

Fiancé. With all his mighty, the Chief Elephant ran towards the Crocodile and almost crushed his head, but the Crocodile realized quickly that the Chief Elephant was very angry and would hurt him. He let go of the Chief Elephant's daughter in time to avoid a very strong kick from the Chief Elephant. It was when the Chief Elephant and his daughter were leaving the pool area that the Chief Elephant saw Tortoises. He went to thank them for sending the message quickly to alert him. He realized that any delay could have resulted in the death of his daughter.

The animals that had gathered near the pool were whispering amongst themselves saying that the Tortoise had gone to warn the Chief Elephant, but that he rejected the warning, chased the Tortoise away and was almost trampled upon.

The other animals concluded by using the proverb that **"He who does not accept advice only realized an axe in his head"**. Other animals knew exactly what the real problem was; the Chief Elephant refused to heed the advice.

A Facial Friend

This proverb is used to warn young people to be careful with some of their friends. Adults would tell young people that some friends were only friends when in their sight but once absent, would either be saying bad things or even planning to hurt them. Adults urge young people to have fewer friends so they can study them and know their sincerity.

To explain this proverb, stories are told and one of them is:

Once upon a time, it is believed that Kalulu and the Hyena were friends and were good dancers in the community. However, although Kalulu was not better than the Hyena, he always wanted to steal the show. At the time, Hyena was known to have been very handsome and skillful in dancing. Kalulu befriended the Hyena so he could always be wherever Hyena was hired. Due to Kalulu's desire to be the best, he would try to use various dancing styles. Kalulu would invite and encourage the audience to join him as this made him more energetic. While dancing, Kalulu would take note of those that seemed unwilling to do what he wanted them do. In most cases Kalulu would aim at the Hyena, whom he wanted to embarrass.

One day Kalulu was hired and not the Hyena. Kalulu decided to invite his friend Hyena with a view to embarrass him in front of other animals. The Hyena did not know Kalulu's hidden intentions as Kalulu would always smile in the face of the Hyena. Whenever Kalulu was dancing, he noted those animals he saw were not doing as requested and would plan on dealing with them in one way of the other. On this day, being the main dancer, he asked other animals, including the Hyena, to perform some maneuvers. Unfortunately, the Hyena did not do as per Kalulu's request. Kalulu developed a grudge against the Hyena and aimed at teaching him a lesson for the disobedience.

One day the Lion King's daughter was getting married. The Lion planned to have a very big wedding celebration. In his planning, Lion thought of having many activities including dancing. He decided to invite the two well-known dancers of the time, Kalulu and the Hyena. The invitation by the King made Kalulu excited as he knew there would be a lot of animals in attendance. He wanted to ensure that his popularity grew even further.

As the Lion was the King, a lot of animals attended the wedding that it was very difficult for other animals to find sitting places. Although the Lion had cleared a very large area, some animals still had to stay outside the arena as more animals than anticipated attended the wedding.

When the time came for dancing, the Lion called upon the Hyena to perform the first dance. All the animals moved forward to get a good view of the show. The Hyena wanted to be noticed by the King and other animals. He performed with all his mighty such that he raised so much dust that excited the animals watching. Many animals clapped and whistled to acknowledge his skill in dancing.

After a while, the Lion motioned to the animals to be quiet, and asked the Hyena to take a rest. He called on the Kalulu to perform a dance too. Kalulu knew that he needed to do better if the animals were to consider him a better dancer than the Hyena. As was his custom, he first bowed to the King and to the other animals, a sign of appreciating their presence. Kalulu started to dance and did his usual tricks. However, the whistling and clapping from the audience was not as much as what the Hyena had received. To spice the dance, he invited the Hyena to come in so they could perform together, but the Hyena refused stating he was tired and needed a few more minutes of rest. Hyena's refusal did not please Kalulu who developed a bigger grudge against him. Kalulu did all his tricks, but the round of applause did not compare to that of the Hyena.

When the wedding celebrations came to an end, Kalulu sought audience with the Hyena. He subtly congratulated the Hyena for the excellent performance and offered to add to what the King had given him in appreciation for his performance. Kalulu told the Hyena that he wanted to surprise him with the gift and would not tell him what it was. Thinking that Kalulu was a true friend, he accepted the offer. Kalulu told the Hyena that he needed three days to prepare the gift. A date and time was set for the Hyena to receive a surprise gift from Kalulu.

When the two parted company, Kalulu went straight to the bush and started to dig a hole. Kalulu wanted to punish the Hyena for refusing to do what he had asked him to do and for seemingly performing better than him. Kalulu's plan was to hurt the Hyena by causing him fall into a deep hole. When he finished digging the hole, Kalulu placed weak sticks on top and covered it with soil so that the hole could not be seen.

When the day came, the Hyena told his family that he was going to collect his gift from Kalulu. His wife was not comfortable with the offer, but Hyena insisted and stated that Kalulu was a good friend and that he showed genuine happiness with the way he had danced.

When the Hyena saw Kalulu, he could not see anything being carried by him. He, however thought that the gift must have been too big to carry and that Kalulu had left it somewhere. Kalulu happily greeted the Hyena and told him that the gift was so special that he had to hide it in the bush. The reason for hiding it was to avoid him being followed when given the gift. He however told Hyena that since it was a surprise gift, he needed to walk backwards when near where the gift was hidden. Kalulu told Hyena that he should follow his instructions until when told to turn around to see the gift.

When the two reached near where Kalulu had dug the hole, he told Hyena to stop as they were near where the gift was. He pointed towards the direction where Hyena was to walk in reverse. Kalulu told the Hyena to move backwards with his eyes closed. The Hyena followed Kalulu's instructions while his heartbeat increased as he visualized a very beautiful gift.

As the Hyena moved in reverse with his eyes closed, he could not see that the area he was approaching had been tampered with. Suddenly the Hyena lost balance and experienced a free-fall. He landed hard at the bottom of the hole on his hind-legs and back. Before he realized what was going on he lost consciousness Kalulu ran away and never stopped to see what had happened to his friend.

The Hyena lay in the hole for most of the day. Hyena's wife got worried when she noticed that her husband had not come back. She decided to follow and ask Kalulu where her husband was. As she walked towards Kalulu's residence, she heard some groaning coming from a nearby bush. She went to see who and why someone was groaning. As she got closer to the bush, she realized the groaning was from her husband. When she approached the place, she saw that her husband was in the hole and was seriously injured. She called for help and other animals came and helped lift the Hyena out of the hole.

It took quite a number of days before the Hyena could walk or speak properly. Recovery took many months as he was seriously hurt, both his hind legs and back were broken. Although the Hyena recovered, he remained maimed with his hind legs shorter than the front ones. His walking became uneven and all his handsomeness was gone. It is believed that since then the Hyena lost his beauty and the ability to dance. The one who seemed a friend on the face was, in reality, an enemy.

Adults use this proverb when they see that their children are not seeing any warning signs in their friends' behaviours; some of them may be *'friends on the face'* while in reality they may be planning to destroy or hurt them.

Know The Song

This proverb is used to encourage young people not to get discouraged by what others may say about them, especially when they seem to face a lot of challenges in life. The young people are encouraged to look at themselves and try to find and develop any hidden talent or skill that they may have. The elders usually tell young people that trying to compare themselves with others will only lead to their being discouraged or depressed. Young people are told that a 'song' is something that may not be known by others, such as a hidden talent. Just like singing requires much practice to perfect it, so should a child spend much time working at developing their unique talents.

To illustrate this proverb, adults tell many stories like the one below:

Once upon a time, when animals and people could communicate with each other, there was a village called Mwase, which had very lovely people. The people loved each other and would do various activities together. As the people and animals could communicate with each other, animals began to share with people their wisdom and knowledge. This type of communication enabled people to gain special knowledge from the animals.

One day a family within the community had a baby boy. Rumor started spreading around that the boy was too ugly to live, and everyone in the village did not want to see it. Some people in the community attributed the ugliness of the boy to the parents having done something wrong and were being punished for it. There were also those who started to advise the family to get rid of the baby before it grew as it was likely to face difficulties in life socially. However, the parents did not heed these pieces of advice and went to seek counsel from the Tortoise. At the time, most people knew that the Tortoise was a well-known Doctor and knew how to treat various ailments. He was also considered to be very wise and was always frequented by those wanting counsel.

The family decided to seek Tortoise's wise counsel as the pressure to get rid of the child was increasing every day. When the family visited the Tortoise, they found him busy with other counsel-seekers. The family decided to wait as they did not want to miss an opportunity of seeing the Tortoise for guidance. They feared that some people could easily harm the baby if they did not put in place adequate strategies to keep it safe. They wanted to know what strategies to put in place and what to do in the long term.

After what seemed to be a week of waiting, the family had an opportunity to see the Tortoise. They narrated their story and asked Tortoise what he thought would be a good plan of action. The Tortoise requested the family to give him a few hours to think through as he had not dealt with something of that type before. The family agreed and went outside to wait again.

After what appeared to be an endless wait, the family was finally called in to see the Tortoise again. When the family had settled in front of the Tortoise, he first started by clearing his throat. He then faced the family and said *"Yours is truly a very rare and difficult matter. I, however, want to commend you as a family for your courage to keep the baby and to seek counsel. I wish to encourage you to keep the baby. Although this may be difficult for you all, you need to know that this baby being unique, will also bring unique opportunities to the family. As the boy grows, urge him to know the 'song'"*. The family did not understand what knowing the song meant and asked the Tortoise to explain what the meaning was. The Tortoise said it slowly; *'Tell the baby as he grows that "When you are ugly you should know the 'song'"*. With this statement, the Tortoise looked into the sky before staring at the family again. He saw that the family was confused. The Tortoise told the family to bring the boy back to him when he is able to understand what is being said. The family asked Tortoise how they will know that age; Tortoise said: *'When the baby begins to ask them the meaning of the statement'*. The family left the

Tortoise's premises with a lot of questions in their heads but accepted Tortoise's counsel.

Although the family accepted the Tortoise's wise counsel, their life became very difficult while looking after the child. Many people in the village stopped associating with the family. The family however, persevered and continued to care for the child while reminding themselves to assist the child to know the 'song'. When the child started to ask the family what was meant by 'knowing the song', the parents knew that their child had reached the right age to be taken back to the Tortoise.

The family took the child back to the Tortoise's place, and waited for their turn to see him. When the family was ushered in and settled, the Tortoise praised them and said he had heard of all the challenges they faced while caring for the boy. He told them that the difficulties were going to be a thing of the past and the boy were to live independently; something that raised more questions in their heads. They could not imagine how that was to happen especially that their boy did not have any friend among his peers. The Tortoise requested the family to leave the boy with him for some time. The family members did not waste time in accepting the request as it was a relief to them. They did not even ask how long the Tortoise wanted to keep the boy for.

When they left, the Tortoise told the boy that he was going to teach him the 'song'. The boy took it that the Tortoise literally meant the actual song. The Tortoise would wake up the boy very early in the morning each day and go with him into the bush to pick various leaves and roots for treating people and other animals that came to him for treatment. He was made to carry heavy bags of medicines which made him feel more unwanted. He thought the Tortoise was being cruel to him as he had nowhere to go. The Tortoise read his thoughts and sat him down. After the conversation, the boy realized that the Tortoise was not being cruel but was teaching him to become a medicine man. The Tortoise also explained to the boy the meaning of 'knowing the song'. This motivated the boy to work very hard. The Tortoise was happy with the way the boy was conducting himself. The Tortoise made the boy take an oath to keep any knowledge leant and skills acquired from him a secret. He was not to disclose anything even to his own parents.

After a few years of the boy being away, his village experienced a problem that no one had an answer for. The people started having tumor-like structures developing on their bodies. The swellings were very painful, and after a period of about a week the swellings would burst and produce smelly pus. The problem became so serious that the King called all Witch Doctors in the area to see if they could find the treatment. After all the attempts by various Witch Doctors failed to produce any positive results, the people became very desperate. Many people suspected witchcraft and pointed fingers at elderly people in their village. The people's allegations against the elderly caused anxiety and stresses among the elderly people and their families.

One day, the Tortoise called the unwanted boy, who at this time was a young adult. The Tortoise asked the boy what he thought of the problem being experienced by the people in his village. The boy responded by telling the Tortoise that other than elders being suspected to be the source of the illness that had affected a lot of people in the village, he too, was being suspected and that there were people plotting to kill him. The Tortoise was saddened with the boy's answer. He told and assured the boy that his life was going to be better and that everyone will be seeking him; not to kill him but to receive his special services. He was to be the only person with knowledge on treating the strange illness. The Tortoise went ahead to explain to the boy how to administer the treatment and that he was to keep the treatment process a secret to himself.

The boy left the Tortoise's place and went straight to his family in the village. He did not reveal to them what he learnt from the Tortoise. In the evening of the same day he arrived in his village, he prepared his medicine and invited a few of his family members, who were sick, to his place. He administered the medicine and told them to go to their houses and to let him know the following day how they would be feeling. The following day, all the family members that received the treatment were healed and had no signs they had tumors on their bodies.

No sooner had the family members narrated the disappearance of the swellings after receiving treatment from the unwanted boy than the people in the village flocked to the boy's home wanting to receive the treatment. The boy told the people to see him in the afternoon as he needed to prepare more medicine.

By the afternoon, the boy's place was crowded with many people wanting to get treated. Although most of the people that came to the boy's house were sick, a few came to just prove what they heard was true. The boy administered the medicine to the people who had gathered at his place and asked them to return to their homes. The following morning all the people that had received the treatment were healed and showed no symptoms of the swellings. The swellings had dried and no scars could be seen.

The news of people being healed from the strange disease spread very quickly to the whole Kingdom and reached the King. The King immediately sent the Messengers to collect the boy from his village in order to administer his medicine to all the royal family members. The King's family received the treatment the very day the boy arrived at the palace upon being summoned. The following day, all the King's family members were healed. This made the King happy, and he praised the boy. As a sign of appreciation, the King ordered that a house and servants be given to the boy so he could easily perform his healing sessions.

The boy's fame spread far and wide that even those that had been plotting to kill him sought to befriend him. All the girls in the villages forgot that this was the very boy they did not want to hear his name mentioned near them, but instead they admired him. Other girls openly made advances towards him for marriage. The boy's status had changed, and he suddenly became rich from presents brought to him by the people he healed. He also charged a fee on all the people he treated.

The boy did not forget what the Tortoise told him about 'knowing the song if ugly'. He went back to the Tortoise's place to thank him. When he arrived at the place, he found that the Tortoise and his family had left, and no one knew where they went. The boy realized that the presence of the Tortoise was not coincidental, but a way in which his life was to be preserved.

Although the boy's appearance had not changed, he was admired by all the people in the Kingdom because he knew what others did not know; the '**song**', being treatment for the unique illness . His knowing what nobody else knew made everybody forget their dislike for him.

When the people in the Kingdom were talking about the unwanted boy, and how suddenly he was the envy of everyone, they used the proverb, '*When ugly know the song'*.

Consequences of Pride

This proverb is usually used to warn young people with a unique talent or skill not to look down on others. The young people are encouraged to know that their talents are to be used for the benefit of the communities. The adults would warn young ones that boasting because of a special talent only created enemies. Humility is the main emphasis on those with unique talents.

To illustrate how a boastful talented young person could destroy themselves, and to explain the meaning of the proverb, adults tell stories like the one below:

Once upon a time when dogs are said to have had horns, and chickens could fly, the Frogs were said to have had excellent voices, and were very good singers. Many animals admired Frogs' singing skills and would spend hours listening to them sing. There was, however, one Frog that had a golden voice. He topped all other Frogs with his golden voice in singing and was the talk in every homestead. He was always the preferred invitee to many gatherings, such as parties and weddings.

With the increased popularity also came the pride. He started to look down on other animals. This behavior became very prominent that other animals disliked the Frog. However, because of his golden voice, they kept inviting him to sing at various functions.

With the increased number of animals developing dislike for the Frog, gossips spread far and wide. Other animals started thinking of ways to discipline the Frog. Kalulu was the one leading the group and worked tirelessly to find a better plan to teach the Frog a lesson.

At one of the events where he was invited, the Frog started boasting after singing beautifully before the crowd. The owner of the function served the Frog with a lot of beer, which he did not want to share with anyone. Kalulu saw that the Frog liked the beer that used a bamboo straw to drink. He devised a plan to teach the boasting Frog a lesson. Kalulu boiled the beer and put in a bamboo straw and told his brother to serve it on the Frog when he motions to him. He told the brother not to let anyone get near the calabash for fear they could detect that the beer in the calabash was hot.

Kalulu went before the crowd and announced to the crowd that he wanted to challenge the Frog on who could drink the beer in the calabash faster. He proposed to offer a big price if the Frog drunk the beer quicker than him. The Frog welcomed the challenge and thought of it as another way he could become more famous. He boastfully declared himself a winner, even before the competition commenced, and called on the Kalulu to come forward as soon as was possible. The Frog first mockingly laughed at Kalulu due to his pride, and talked him down.

The two calabashes were brought, one by the brother to Kalulu, which was placed in front of the Frog, and another in front of Kalulu. However, because of his pomposity, the Frog went straight and took hold of the straw even before a go sign was given. He took a deep breath and after expelling the air off his chest, he drew on the straw with all his mighty to finish the brew in one pull.

The Frog pulled with all his mighty, but because the brew was still boiling and very hot, the strong pull gushed the hot brew into Frog's throat. The Frog suddenly jumped into the air and fell backwards on the ground rolling and holding his throat. Although he wanted to shout, he could not, as there was no sound coming out of his mouth. Other animals first thought the Frog was just joking by jumping into the air and falling on his back. When they saw that the Frog was not producing any sound, they realized something must have happened to the Frog, but did not understand what exactly it was. The Frog could neither swallow nor spit out the hot beer; it was stuck into his throat. He collapsed and fainted. As soon as he saw the Frog jump into the air and fall on his back, Kalulu disappeared into the crowd with both calabashes of beer.

When other animals realized the seriousness of what happened to the Frog, they quickly managed to clear his throat, but was unable to speak as the whole throat was swollen. His vocal cords were seriously scalded. The Frog rushed to the water to try and cool his throat as the heat in his throat was unbearable. The Frog remained near the water so he could keep cooling his throat for a long time. The Frog was unable to speak or sing for a long time.

When the Frog finally recovered, he could no longer sing as before. He also experienced consistent heat in his throat and stayed near the water forever. Each time the frog sees water, he goes into it to cool his throat, and then tries to sing again. But each time he tries to sing, his voice fails, and he croaks the whole time. He continues trying to sing, hoping to get his golden voice back.

Whenever elders see a young person or any community member being boastful, they cite the proverb, 'Pride cost the Frog his golden voice'.

The Grey-Haired Person

IF TODAY A GREY-HAIRED PERSON DISAPPEARS, AND
THE FOLLOWING DAY GREY HAIR IS FOUND IN HY-
ENA'S POO OR FAECES, WHAT WOULD YOU SAY HAP-
PENED TO THE GREY-HAIRED PERSON?

Although this sounds like a question, it is a proverb that assists hearers to make own conclusions on what they hear is being said to them. The elders would ask this proverbial question to urge the listeners to connect facts before them to what they either understand could have happened or make their own conclusion. The proverb is based on the inability of the Hyenas to digest some hard stuff such as hair. The Hyena's poo is said to contain some of the food it ate a day or two previously. However, grey hair is usually unique to old people. If an old person in a village disappears and grey hair is noticed in the Hyena's poo, they usually conclude that the Hyena ate the old person. The strong association of the disappearance of the grey-haired person and the presence of grey hair in the Hyena's poo is usually very correct and accurate.

To assist young people to understand this proverb, elders would tell stories such as the one below:

A long time ago in a certain village was a very handsome young man who did not want to learn how to do any manual work. He was so proud of his handsomeness that he paid much attention to his outlook and what everyone in the village would say about him. He thought he could lose his handsomeness if he engaged in any form of manual work. Although the parents did everything to explain to him that failure to know how to perform certain chores could work against him in future, the boy did not heed this as he felt his handsomeness was the solution to his future problems, especially that most of the girls in the village, and surrounding areas, wanted very much to befriend him.

With passage of time, days became weeks, weeks became months and months became years. The boy also grew and reached the adolescent stage. With him reaching the marrying age, the boy started thinking of finding a girl to marry. The parents were not in favor of him marrying as they knew their boy was going to fail to support the wife, and that he would eventually bring shame upon the family. To avoid facing such an embarrassment the family discouraged any young girl they would see getting closer to their son. Eventually a lot of people in the nearby and surrounding villages became aware that despite being handsome, the boy was lazy and most likely to fail to look after his wife.

The boy quickly realized that chances of getting a girl to marry in his community were non-existent. He thought of going somewhere far where he was not known. The young man managed to travel to a distant place where he was unknown, and quickly sought a girl to marry. It did not take him long to find a beautiful young lady to marry due to his handsomeness. All wedding arrangements were made without any of his family members being involved by claiming to have come from a very far place and that waiting for his relatives to be involved in the marriage arrangements was going to delay the wedding arrangements. The people believed him and went ahead with marriage arrangements, and then the wedding celebrations.

The family of the girl was excited and did everything to support the new couple; they arranged for their honeymoon too. Everyone on the bride's side was happy that their daughter had married a handsome young man that everyone in the area admired.

All the excitement settled down after few months and the family members expected the couple to start living like any other family. As was normally the case in those days, his wife expected her husband to lead in the raising of the income for the family. However, the boy did not only spend most of his time in the house sleeping, but also did nothing else, let alone slashing the grass around the house. With time, his wife got agitated with him as she did almost all the chores in and outside their home.

As pressure grew on this young man from his wife to be the husband like all others, he devised plans to show that he could look after her. He told his wife that he was used to working at night. When he told her this, he started disappearing from the house every evening, and only returned in the early hours of the morning, just before dawn. He would return with a lot of fresh meat and some food. The wife, being unsuspecting, would receive the food and the meat, and arrange them nicely in the house.

After a while, rumors started going around that many people in the area were losing their livestock such as goats, pigs, and chickens. Women stopped leaving their food outside to dry, as they would find most of the it gone in the morning. Since the wife did not suspect anything, she was even proudly telling other women of the meat and food her husband was bringing home, and how that she had more than enough to live on. Somehow, people started suspecting him of being the thief, but could not openly accuse him due to lack of evidence.

With the increase in the food and livestock missing and rumors about the suspected thief, the village headmen decided to call for a meeting so the villages could devise ways of catching the thief. The meeting was called and almost all the villages attended. The deliberations took almost the whole day as each person had his or her own suggestion to make. There were so many propositions and counter propositions that they almost adjourned the meeting without reaching a consensus. A lot of people, including the young handsome man, were asked to account for their day-to-day whereabout. He was able to exculpate himself, and people could not conclusively point a finger at him as the thief.

When hope was almost lost of finding a solution to the problem and reaching a consensus on what was to be done, one person stood up and asked that he be given a few minutes to try and bring everyone to think deeply as to why the villages had found themselves at this crossroad. He first asked the villages to think of anytime in the past that they had any food and livestock missing; everyone shook their heads indicating that they had never experienced such. He then went to address the people, 'While I cannot point my finger at anyone, I would like the people present to think carefully. We need to look at the period we have had this problem. We seem to have had this problem arise in the last couple of months. Secondly, all other villages distant from us are not experiencing a similar problem. To me the problem is a local one, which can be resolved if we can answer this question about the disappearance of grey-haired man and the presence of the grey hair in the Hyena's feaces'.

At this point, people began to nod their heads and looking in the direction of the young man and his wife. The Senior Village headman got the point, but he did not want to accuse the young man due to lack of evidence. He motioned to the people and addressed them by stating that he seemed to have found a way of resolving the problem. He decided to order all men to be spending the nights at his palace for the following few weeks to see if the problem would continue. All men were to go back to their houses in the morning and do their chores but be expected to return to the palace in the evenings. This was to be trialed for a whole week, after which another meeting was to be held.

During the first three days, although women were encouraged to leave the food outside to dry, there was no one who had lost any food or livestock. However, as per agreement, the Village Headman insisted that the trial should run for the whole week. Again, there were no cases of missing food and livestock the whole week that the men spent the nights at the palace. At the end of the week, all the people gathered again as resolved in the previous meeting. Even though many people had made a connection between the disappearance of their livestock and the coming of the young handsome man, they did not have evidence to single him out as anyone among the men could still have been the thief.

When the meeting was called to order, the senior Village Headman told the people to refer to the question about the disappearance of a grey-haired man and the appearance of grey hair in the Hyena's poo. He stated that the problem of livestock and other food items going missing was a recent one and was linked to men. He stated that his conclusion was based on the outcome of the trial where all men spent the nights at the palace. However, having caught no one and having no cases of theft taking place while all men slept at the Village Headman's palace only confirmed that one of the men was probably the thief.

He urged the people to consider the matter again before leaving the meeting. Despite various suggestions, all the people in the village could not conclusively point the finger at the young handsome man. However, the young man used the meeting to announce his intentions to leave the village with his wife.

The villages did not experience another theft of the livestock or food items since the departure of the handsome young man with his wife. So, the only way the people in the villages concluded the matter was to cite the proverb, *'If today a grey-haired person disappears, and the following day grey hair is found in Hyena's poo or faeces, what would you say happened to the Grey-haired person?'*.

Be Patient

This proverb draws its meaning from the snail's sensitive response to any danger by hiding its eyes. It is usually said that for someone to see the snail's eyes, he/she must be still for a long time near the snail. It is only when the snail does not sense any danger that it opens its eyes. It is assumed that not many people know the location of the snail's eyes.

The proverb is used to encourage young people, even adults, not to rush into conclusion over anything or rush into wanting to get the results quickly from any activity. Young people are encouraged to wait before doing anything, especially when wanting to marry.

To assist young people to remember this proverb adults tell stories like the one below:

Once upon a time there was a very rich King who had many servants. He loved his servants so much that he used to take different ones on different outings. The servants became so royal to their

King as they did not see any favoritism in him. The servants were also so free talking to the King such that people in the kingdom always desired to be one of his servants.

There was one servant among all, who the King liked but did not think his usual use of the proverb that *'one needed to be patient to see the eyes of the snail'*, was of any use to him as the King. He usually wanted things to be done according to his commands. He would get upset whenever the servant would get back to the King and advise him to wait if the servant thought what the King wanted to be done did not warrant urgent action, or if urgent action ordered by the King would not yield the best outcome.

As time went by, the King kept waiting to see if what this servant was saying really had any relevance to his life. One day he asked this servant to accompany him on a hunting trip. They went into the jungle and camped there for a while, something that used to happen in those days, as hunters would travel long distances away from the villages. This used to be the practice as hunting parties would make their kills and also dry the meat before returning. There were no fridges or deep freezers in those days, and the only way to preserve the meat was by drying it.

One day while still on this hunting spree, the King wanted to make the last kill, before returning to the Palace. He called the servant that liked to use the proverb to accompany him and left all others behind. When they just left the camp, they were attacked by the Lion. The Lion targeted the King. The servant was quick to act and killed the Lion before any serious harm was inflicted on the King. However, the Lion had mauled the King's hand and the King lost the thumb during the struggle. The King started bleeding profusely, but the servant quickly stopped the bleeding. The King was upset seeing that he had lost his thumb. The servant, once again, told the King that he needed not to worry but to patiently wait and see the reason for his being attacked, as there could be a purpose for what had just happened. The King asked the servant to explain the meaning of all that, but the servant reminded the king to remember that seeing the eyes of the snail required patience. Although the King calmed down, he did not agree with what the servant said to him.

After a few months and the King's wound had healed, the King once again decided to undertake another trip to visit some remote parts of his Kingdom. On this occasion, he decided to leave behind the servant who rescued him from the Lion as he thought his use of the proverb would probably annoy him. As the King and his servants journeyed through the bushes, they were attacked and captured by a gang of people that practiced human sacrifice. The servants tried to fight them off, but they were eventually overpowered. The King was also captured and taken into captivity. They were all led away into this people's hideout where they were to be sacrificed.

When the time for sacrificing them came, they were all lined up, including the King himself. When the people to sacrifice them did the inspection, the three servants and the king were found unfit to be sacrificed. The King was unfit to be sacrificed because he was missing a thumb, and so he was set free, together with his other three servants who also had various parts of their body missing. The King and his servants hurriedly went back to their Kingdom. Upon arrival at his palace, the King narrated how they were captured, the four of them released and the rest offered as sacrifice. He commanded that a war be waged against the human-sacrificing group of people. Upon hearing the King's order, the servant who liked to use the proverb about patience to see the snail's eyes, requested to speak to the king before waging the war. The servant reminded the King that *'to see the snail's eyes, one needed to be patient'*. The King became angry and shouted at the servant reminding him of the other servants who had been killed. He demanded that the servant explains to him why all this had happened and the reason he needed to wait before attacking the group. The servant humbly reminded the King what he had said to him at the time he lost his thumb. He also reminded the King that had he been whole, he probably would not have returned as he could have been sacrificed, and that the absence of the thumb was the reason the King was spared. Immediately, the King calmed down and asked his servant to propose the best course of action.

The King was advised to wait before doing anything as the human-sacrificing group would be expecting an attack, and they would be prepared to defend themselves. The King needed to wait for the situation to settle down and then attack when people-sacrificing group was not expecting it. This worked and the king was very happy with his servant's wise counsel. The King started to use the proverb; '*to see the snail's eyes, one must be patient*'.

Stubborn Demands

This proverb is used to warn young people, and others, not to make demands which could have fatal consequences. They are encouraged to appreciate the guidance of the adults who could be telling them of things that they either experienced or witnessed in their lifetime. Young people are urged not to think that what they currently want is good in that they may not have knowledge of the future consequences.

To encourage young people follow the advice of the elders/adults, adults tell stories like the one below:

Once upon a time there was a lovely jungle with plenty of water and food. The jungle attracted so many animals due to the abundant food, water, and other requirements for their livelihood. Many animals found the jungle a desirable place to live in and did not think of moving anywhere else.

Among the animals living in the jungle were the Sables. Sables are relatively large animals with horns curving backwards. The backward-pointing horns make it easy for them to pass through the thickets and to drink water in confined spaces where water holes are found. The disadvantage that Sables face with their horns curving backwards is in their inability to use the horns to fight off their enemies. They cannot use their horns to inflict pain on their enemies. Their predators find it easier to attack and kill the Sables; they are defenseless

In one of the Sable family a young male saw that most of the Sables were unable to defend themselves against their enemies. He decided to change the orientation of his horns. He knew that by treating the horns while they grew would change their orientation and point forward. With the horns pointing forward, he would defend himself against the predators during the attack. He told his parents about his plans to have the orientation of his horns altered so they could face forward to easily defend himself. His parents explained to him that while he was likely to defend himself, he will be facing difficulties finding his way through the thickets, hence reducing his chances of escaping from his enemies. The parents' explanations did not convince the young male Sable who decided to ignore his parents' advice.

As soon as the horns emerged on his head, the young Sable sought the services of the horns-curator, who happened to be Mr. Warthog. The young Sable admired the outward stretched horns of the

Warthog that he used to tear off some tree-barks, and even to defend himself against the enemies. The Warthog started working on the young Sable's horns so that they did not curve backwards. The process was long, but the young Sable was determined to achieve his goal, especially when he thought that he could easily challenge his peers and send them running away from him. With his horns facing forward, the young Sable was feared among the peers because he could use his horns to inflict injuries on them during the fights.

After some years, the jungle was affected by drought. Many rivers dried and only a few water pools had water in them. The food also became scarce in the jungle. The shortage of food resulted in many animals either dying from starvation or forced migration to distant places to find food. The reduced population of animals in the jungle increased the likelihood of them, like the Sables, being attacked by predators like Hyenas, Lions and Leopards. The young Sable found it really hard to maneuver in the thickets when either avoiding being seen or running away from the enemies. The parents did not want to see their son get killed, so they would lead the way through the thickets and the Young Sable followed them behind. This went on for some time.

The continued drought resulted in many more water pools drying out. However, there was only one place that had a spring of water and had not dried. Many animals flocked to this place to drink. The place was also dangerous as many predators found it ideal for finding their preys. The place was surrounded by rocks and had a narrow passage leading to the water hole. The animals had to squat and lower their heads to reach the water at the bottom of the hole. Due to the high risk of being caught by predators, the animals had to drink as quickly as possible and then run to a safer distance.

The young Sable went to the same place with his parents and friends to drink too. However, he could not reach the water because his horns would hit the walls of the passage preventing him from lowering the head to reach the water level. The Young Sable tried all he could, but his horns proved a big barrier to reach the water. The young Sable spent a lot of time trying to get to the water but could not manage. The more he tried to reach the water without success, the weaker he became due to dehydration. As he continued to try to reach the water, he did not see the enemies closing in on him. The parents shouted to warn the young Sable of the impending danger. The Young Sable tried to run away from the predators but could not manage to run as he was too dehydrated and weak. The predators easily caught him, and he could not fight them off as he had no strength left in him. His parents shouted from a distance telling their son that had he listened to their advice, he would not have died.

Other animals that were listening, including his friends, understood that his stubborn demands were the cause of his death; '*The young Sable died of thirst*'.

Don't Insult the Crocodile

DO NOT INSULT THE CROCODILE WHILE YOUR FEET
ARE STILL IN THE WATER

This proverb is used when adults see that either their friends or young people are demeaning those providing essential services, or are bad-mouthing people or service-providers before they are weaned from such services. It warns the young people that by talking ill of those people assisting them, they may lose out should those people decide to discontinue assisting them.

To teach young people to appreciate assistance being rendered to them, adults in my village would tell stories such as the one below. The context is that of old days, when most rivers would start flowing during the rainy season. As these streams would only have water flowing during the rainy seasons, they would have no bridges. People would cross them by wadding through the water. Occasionally, Crocodiles would also stray into these streams. So, people were encouraged not to speak ill of Crocodiles while they were still crossing the stream.

A long, long, time ago, when animals lived in harmony with each other, it is said that the Lion and the Hyena were good friends. The two families used to share a lot of things, including caring for each other's young ones. Usually, the Lions would leave their Cubs with the Hyenas whenever they went hunting. In return, the Hyena family would receive some meat from the Lions. In other instances, the two families would go hunting together, and once the Lions had a kill and were satisfied, the Hyenas would then enjoy the left-over meat. Their friendship blossomed so well that other animals admired the relationship.

With time, the Lions began to experience difficulties finding animals to kill near where they lived. They began to cover long distances before they could find their preys. When the Lioness gave birth to four Cubs and could not take them along when going to hunt, they decided to seek the assistance of the Hyenas to look after the Cubs. The Cubs were also too small to accompany the parents when hunting. The Lions continued asking the Hyena family to care for their Cubs each time they went hunting. The Hyenas would take the Cubs into their Caves until their parents returned.

The Lions continued to experience difficulties finding the animals in the nearby areas. In some instances, they would be gone for three or four days. Later, the Lions began to take longer before returning with the meat for their Cubs. The delayed returns would put pressure on the Hyenas to find alternative food for themselves and for the Cubs.

One day the Lion family left their Cubs with the Hyena family and told the Hyena to sparingly give the remaining meat to their Cubs as they were not certain of their return. The Hyena assured the Lions not to worry but that his family would do everything possible to safeguard the wellbeing of the Cubs. However, the Cubs were growing up very quickly and their meat consumption was increasing too. The Lions' delays in returning with the meat meant that Hyenas had to find alternative sources of meat for the Cubs and themselves, and they really struggled to satisfy the Cubs.

At another time when the Lions returned, the Cubs complained to their parents, alleging that Hyenas consumed most of the meat and were not receiving enough to satisfy their hunger. The Lions became unhappy and threatened to discipline the Hyenas. The Lions further threatened to kill the Hyenas' children should their Cubs not receive enough meat next time they went out hunting. The Hyenas were extremely disappointed but could not do anything against the Lions. The Hyenas could also not walk away from the Lions as they did not have good hunting skills to provide meat for themselves and their children. However, they vowed to deal with the Lions' Cubs should they be asked to look after them again.

After some days had passed, the Lions ran out of meat and needed to go hunting again. The Cubs were still too young to be taken along on the long hunting trips. The Lions went back to the Hyenas and asked if they could care for the Cubs while they went hunting. The Hyenas accepted the request and brought the Cubs into their cave.

The Lions did not return with the meat for a long time. The animals had migrated to very distant places. The Hyenas ran out of meat for the Cubs. The Cubs started to put pressure on the Hyenas to give them the meat. The Hyenas thought of solving the problem in a subtle way; they killed one of the Cubs in the night and gave the meat to the remaining three Cubs. The Cubs did not think of their missing sibling as they were very hungry. They ate the meat and straight away fell asleep.

No sooner had the Cubs slept than the Lions arrived with some meat. The Lions were in a hurry to return as they had sighted some animals nearby on their return. They wanted to make a kill before the animals went very far. They called on the Hyenas to just show them the Cubs and to quickly come out of their cave to get the meat for the Cubs. The Hyenas felt a sense of relief as they were not sure how to respond to the Lions if they asked about the whereabout of the other Cub. The Hyena lifted the first Cub and showed it to the Lyons. He put the Cub down and lifted the second one. He did the same with the third one. He then lifted up the first one and shouted to the Lions that the four Cubs were safe. The

Lions turned round and rushed back to find the animals they had seen.

The animals that the Lions had seen had also seen the Lions. As soon as the Lions had disappeared from their sight, the animals ran as fast as they could so that the Lions could not find them. The Lions ran and ran but could not find the animals. They again had to stay much longer as they could not find the animals to kill near the cave where the Hyenas and the Cubs were.

After a few days, the three Cubs consumed all the meat and were again demanding that the Hyenas give them more. The Hyenas got the second Cub and killed it in the night as before. There was meat for the remaining two Cubs. The Cubs ate the meat for few days before their parents returned with more meat. The Lions did not want to stay long again this time, so they asked the Hyena to show them the Cubs like the previous time. The Hyena was relieved again. He lifted the first Cub and showed it to the Lions. He then put the Cub down before lifting the second one. He then lifted the first one again and did the same with the second one, seemingly showing four Cubs to the Lions. The Lions took off again to find more meat for the Cubs. The Lions were certain that they will carry their Cubs in the next hunting trip as the Cubs looked bigger and stronger.

The Lions took much longer before bringing the meat to the Hyenas for the Cubs. The Hyenas ran out of meat again. So, the two Cubs, who were now much bigger, started to harass the Hyenas.

The Hyenas waited until the Cubs had slept before pouncing on one of them. They killed it and brought the meat to the remaining Cub. The remaining Cub ate the meat and was happy as there was no competition when eating the meat. The Hyenas were worried as they did not know what to do if the Lions demanded to see their four Cubs, but also that the Lions were most likely going to stay longer before going back hunting.

The Hyena sent his family away to the other caves. He remained alone with the Cub. As soon as he had settled, he heard the roaring of the Lions. The Hyena knew that they had come back with a lot of meat. The Lions called the Hyena to come out and assist carrying some of the meat into the cave for the Cubs and for his family. They also quickly told the Hyena that they were going to stay longer before returning to hunt. The Hyena left the remaining Cub in the corner of the Cave and went out to carry the meat. The Lions were entering the cave when the Hyena was going out, pretending to rush to bring in the meat. Once outside, the Hyena did not waste any time before taking off at great speed running away and hid himself in another cave.

The Lions called their Cubs but only one showed up. The Lions then called the Hyena, but the Hyena did not answer. The Lions went outside the cave to see what was happening that the Hyena was not responding. To their dismay, there was no sign of the Hyena. The Lions suspected that something had gone wrong, they quickly went back into cave where they saw blood in one of the corners of the cave. They realized that their Cubs had been killed by the Hyenas. The Lions started to roar, they roared so loud that the Leopards and the Cheetahs came to see why the Lions were roaring so loud and seemed to be in grief. The Lions explained the situation to the Leopards and the Cheetahs.

On hearing what the Lions narrated, they realized that the Lions had been threatening the Hyenas even though they knew that they had nowhere else to leave their Cubs. So, the Leopards and Cheetahs did not say much fearing being attacked by the Lions.

Later when away from the Lions, they started talking among themselves about the way Hyenas were being harassed by the Cubs, and how the Lion did not support the Hyenas but instead also threatened to kill their children. They wondered how the Lions could expect the Hyenas to perform a good job under threats. In concluding their conversation, they cited the proverb, 'Do not insult the Crocodile while your feet are still in water'.

Thighs of an Elephant

The Elephant is a very large animal barely with any space between its thighs. It is, therefore, almost impossible for someone to pass through its thighs without being squeezed to death. If one manages to pass through the thighs of an elephant, they are thought to be extremely luck, and are urged not to make another attempt as likelihood of surviving is also extremely slim.

The proverb is used to warn someone who survives a very serious incident. Anyone or young person that survives a very serious incident is usually urged to avoid exposing themselves to similar events. In the village setup, events of surviving a Python attack is considered a rare occurence, and anyone that survives such an attack is discouraged from frequenting the rivers infested with large water-Pythons and Crocodiles.

To explain the proverb, adults in the villages tell stories such as the one below:

A long time ago in a certain village lived a very beautiful girl. Most men had tried to win her hand in marriage but failed. The girl had set a very high standard for the would-be husband. While there were many young men who had interest in her, many did not dare approach her for fear of being disappointed. The story of the girl and her demands went everywhere in the Kingdom.

When the story of the girl that made young men fail to marry her spread far and wide, it attracted others from distant places. When the Hyena heard of this beautiful girl and how that most young men had failed to win her hand in marriage, he decided to take a chance. The Hyena went to see the Tortoise, who was very famous for his magic, and knew how to change animals into various beings. The Tortoise when approached by the Hyena, did not hesitate to assist the Hyena become a human being. He, however, warned the Hyena to strictly follow certain rules to remain a human. The Hyena promised to follow the instructions as he desired to marry the beautiful girl that had turned down many young men. The Tortoise emphasized to the Hyena the most important rule for him not to eat bones, even when cooked by the girl he intended to marry. He also told the Hyena that the day he ate the bones that will be the day he will revert back into a Hyena. The Tortoise urged the Hyena to heed his warning as the process could not be reversed.

The Hyena, who was now in form of a very handsome young man, took a journey to the village where the girl lived. The girl and the people in the village were impressed and wondered where the young man came from, as they had not seen him in their Kingdom before. The young man, formerly the Hyena, told them that his name was Manjata, and that he had come from a very far country. He told the girl and her parents that he had heard of the beautiful girl from his people that had visited the village and wanted to ask the girl's hand in marriage.

As the girl was already impressed and interested in the young man the very first time she saw him, just like her parents, the negotiations did not take long to conclude. The parents accepted Manjata to marry their daughter. They however, asked for Manjata to bring in his relatives to finalise the wedding arrangements. However, Manjata told them that it would take a long time for his relatives to arrive to their village and get involved in the wedding arrangements. He pleaded with the girl's parents to allow him finalize all the arrangements without his relatives, alleging that he could not imagine himself spending a few more weeks without the girl of his dream. The parents accepted Manjata's explanations as they did not want to disappoint their daughter, who was also keen to get married.

Although some people in the village expressed doubts and concerns about the legitimacy of Manjata's claims about his identity, they did not say anything to the contrary, as they knew there were no young men in the area that had not tried their luck to marry the girl. The marriage arrangements were quickly finalized and a wedding day announced. A lot of people were invited to the wedding ceremony.

The day of the wedding ceremony finally arrived, and people started to gather as early as the darkness cleared. Many people came to the wedding out of curiosity, to see how the young man that had managed to win the heart of the 'difficult' girl looked like. Others came to the wedding ceremony to see what the groom would be wearing, and what gift the groom was going to present to the bride and her family. Others used the wedding as an opportunity to find their future wives and husbands.

There were many dancing groups and performers to spice the wedding day. Most of the dancers were hired by the bride's family who wanted to honor their daughter as she left the family home to start her own. There was also a lot of food and meat to feed the people attending the wedding on the day. The people ate a lot of meat, and as they threw the bones away, a pile could be seen where they were being kept either to feed the dogs or disposal. The sight of bones excited Manjata, as the desire for bones in him had not completely disappeared. Manjata had difficulties keeping himself from drooling with bones being thrown away by the people as they enjoyed themselves. Manjata tried to eat the food being served to them at the high table, but his eyes kept straying towards the pile of bones.

When the wedding activities had finished, and all celebrations concluded, it was time for the newly wed to go to their house to rest. Manjata kept drooling at the sight of bones, which he almost picked as he and the bride walked to their house. When the bride asked Manjata why he tried to pick the bones, he told her that he just wanted to throw them away stating that he feared stepping on them. The wife did not suspect anything, and so they proceeded walking to the house. Manjata had noticed the site where the people had thrown the bones. He imagined himself sitting near the heap, when he was suddenly interrupted by the bride asking him to usher her into the house. Although he went into the house, his attention was on the pile of bones he had seen, and his desire for them became unbearable.

When the bride had slept and the village was quiet, Manjata tip-toed out of the house and went to the rubbish pit where he found a heap of bones. He picked a lot of them, and quickly tip-toed back into the house. He went straight into the spare bedroom where he put them into a container. At first, he resisted the temptation to eat the bones on rememberingthe warning from the Tortoise. He went back to the bedroom where his bride was, still fast asleep. However, the smell of the bones from another bedroom made it difficult for Manjata to fall asleep. Eventually, when he could not stand it any longer, he again tip-toed to the other bedroom and immediately started to crush the bones.

Manjata had eaten almost half of the pile of bones when he realized that he was turning back into a Hyena, and his voice was had changed. He tried to hide the voice by coughing, but that woke up the bride from sleep. She called him when she did not feel him in bed. Manjata tried to respond, but instead of the voice, he was whooping (laughing). The bride was alarmed thinking that the Hyena had trespassed into their house. She called aloud for Manjata, but the whooping became even louder. The bride screamed aloud calling for help. The people who had spent a night in the village after the wedding heard the calling for help from the new couple's house.

When the bride opened the door to escape from the Hyena, fearing that her husband could have been injured by the Hyena, Manjata took advantage of the open door to escape from the house for safety. The people who were running towards the house saw a Hyena running from the house. They chased after it, but because it was dark, they could not see where the Hyena had run to. After a while, they heard the laughter of the Hyena from a distance. Some people went into the house to check for Manjata, who the bride thought was in the house probably injured. They did not find Manjata but found a hip of bones in the other bedroom and Manjata's clothes on the floor. They started to suspect that Manjata could have been the Hyena they saw running away from the house.

When the situation calmed down, people gathered around the parents and the bride, and told them that they suspected Manjata to be the Hyena they had seen running away from the house. At first, the bride refused to believe them, and wanted to go to look for Manjata. She thought the Hyenas could have dragged him along with them. The people and the parents told the girl that Manjata could easily have killed her if what the people were saying was the truth. She needed to heed the advice being given to her. They concluded that if Manjata was the Hyena, and was allowed to come back, she most likely would not be able to escape his ferocious attack. The presence of Manjata's clothes in the house proved beyond doubt that Manjata was not really human, but the Hyena they had seen running away from the house. The bride agreed with what the people said and did not argue with her parents anymore.

The parents and people told the girl that she was very lucky that Manjata had not attacked her in the first place, instead went for the bones. The people encouraged the girl to remain with her parents. The girl accepted their advice to remain with the parents. In concluding, the people cited the proverb, '*one cannot go between the thighs of the Elephant twice*'.

A Blind Man

A long time ago, there were two people who became very good friends, and loved each other like brothers. Their names were Kafindondo and Lumpeni. Lumpeni was the older of the two by almost three years. The three-year age difference did not seem to exist as the two looked almost the same age, and their statures were also the same. Some people, who did not know them, thought they were twins. They grew up doing most of things together; they went to look for girls to marry together and eventually got married in the same year. They both had children, and each cared for the other's children as if they were his own. Both Kafindondo and Lumpeni were free to encourage and advise any of their children to be responsible and to work hard to be successful in life.

The two friends were very talented and had a successful lifestyle in line with the village standard at the time. As time passed and children were growing, the two friends decided to go to a distant country to experience a different lifestyle, which they had heard from the friends who lived there talk about. The two friends were always fascinated with the new discoveries and experiences. The stories from friends who lived in that distant country encouraged them to go and see for themselves.

Kafindondo was the first to leave the village. Since Kafindondo had some close relatives in that distant country, he took along with him his family. However, Kafindondo did not contact his friend Lumpeni, as there were no Mobile phones at the time, and the only means to communicate with the people in the village was by hand-written letters. Kafindondo was working long hours and did not find time to write letters to his friend, Lumpeni. The lack of communication from Kafindondo made Lumpeni wonder whether his friend was alright. He, however, comforted himself in that if Kafindondo had any problems he would have heard from the relatives. Lumpeni was one day fortunate to see a picture of his friend, Kafindondo, that he had sent to his relatives. In the picture he looked much healthier and happy. The picture rekindled the desire in Lumpeni to also go and experience life in that distant country. Lumpeni also thought that Kafindondo was not communicating with him because he was having a very comfortable life in the distant country.

Lumpeni worked very hard in that year to raise money for a trip to the distant country, where his friend Kafindondo was. Being uncertain of what life was going to be like in that distant country, Lumpeni discussed with his family and agreed to leave them behind until he found work and accommodation before they could join him. He had also heard that some people in that distant country had become destitutes due to financial challenges. The family and friends were pleased with his wisdom.

Lumpeni finally left the village and travelled to the distant country where Kafindondo had gone. The country was so large that the two did not meet for a long time. However, the two met at one of the functions in the city, and their friendship was rekindled. Living in different cities meant that they could only spend time talking to each other only when at some functions. Unfortunately, the functions were rare, as such they did not see each other often.

Lumpeni managed to find employment and good accommodation. After a while, he sent money for his family to join him. It was after many months that Lumpeni informed his friend of his family finally joining him. Kafindondo travelled to his friend's city to visit his friend's family. They spent the whole day talking about the village lifestyle, and how different things were in the cities of the distant country where they were. After a visit Kafindondo went back to his city. Lumpeni promised to visit his friend once the family settled. Despite the promise, Lumpeni never went to visit his friend even after the family had settled.

With time, both Lumpeni's and Kafindondo's children grew up and completed their education, others started working, but the two friends did not meet. Kafindondo wondered why his friend was not fulfilling his promise to visit his family. This made Kafindondo hesitant to visit his friend and his family at their home.

One day, Kafindondo went for a function, which was in the city where his friend Lumpeni lived. While there, Kafindondo met his friend's children, but Lumpeni himself was not in attendance. Kafindondo was very happy to see his friend's children and spent time happily chatting with them. While Kafindondo was chatting with his friend's children, he started to talk to them about proper conduct while living in the distant country's big city where they were. Kafindondo had lived in this distant country longer than his friend, he thought things were like before, that he could talk to his friend's children as though they were his own. He was unaware that some of the things he was telling the children had actually happened to them, and his friend's children took it that Kafindondo had heard about those things from other people and was now aiming at embarrassing them. The children neither showed their unhappiness nor any negative reactions to show their feelings about what Kafindondo was talking about. The function came to an end and everyone happily left for their homes. After a few days, Kafindondo received a message summoning him to meet his friend and talk about what he said to his children.

Kafindondo did not know what it was all about but did not waste any time to meet his friend. Upon seeing his friend, Lumpeni got aggressive, pointing a threatening finger at him for talking behind his back and bringing up things that he had wanted to forget about; things that had negatively affected him and his children. Lumpeni also wondered why his friend Kafindondo had decided to talk to the children instead of him. Kafindondo was shocked and tried to explain that he did not understand what his friend was talking about. Lumpeni did not accept his friend's explanation, but he instead stringently warned him of dire consequences if he continued talking to the children. He further expressed to Kafindondo of his displeasure about Kafindondo's use of stories gathered from other people about the children.

The onlookers intervened and calmed Lumpeni. They asked Kafindondo what was happening that his friend got so angry with him. Kafindondo explained and stated that he was unaware of the allegations raised against him and the other things he was being accused of. The people believed Kafindondo and realized he had no prior knowledge of the things that his friend's children went through. They also saw that Kafindondo had no intentions to emotionally injure his friend's children. They pleaded with Lumpeni to forgive his friend seeing that he had no prior knowledge of the things that happened the children, especially that Kafindondo lived in another city, far from the city where Lumpeni and his family lived.

After some discussions and explanations, Lumpeni calmed down. In concluding the matter, the elders present told Lumpeni that his friend, Kafindondo, was like a blind person who unknowingly stepped on his foot. So, they used the proverb, '*you do not get angry at the blind man when he steps on your foot*'.

Dance, Rugs and Fire

DO NOT DANCE NEAR THE FIRE IF YOU ARE WEARING
A TATTERED SKIRT

This proverb is based on the flammability of the rugs when exposed to fire, and they can easily catch the fire. The context is that most traditional dances used to take place in the evenings, and there would also be large fires (bonfire) to keep both the dancers and the spectators warm. Those with tattered clothes were discouraged from sitting closer to the fires as embers could easily ignite their loose rugs. In the proverb, the tattered skirt is equated to vulnerability. Many adults and parents knew those that were vulnerable either in the community or the family, respectively, and would discourage them from participating in the activities or events that could hurt them. The vulnerable are usually advised to avoid some activities that could either worsen their problems or increase their vulnerability. In most cases the vulnerable ones would not understand what they were being told. To assist them to walk away and avoid further harm, the adults used the proverb.

To make young people understand the proverb, adults in the village used stories like the one below:

A long time ago there was a Kingdom that had a very big river flowing through it. There was one point along the river that used to get flooded. Whenever the river flooded, at that point there would be a lot of fish floating and were easily caught. Some people decided to build a village near the spot. However, they built their houses on rocks high enough for floods not to wash off their homes. The villagers would catch a lot of fish every time the river flooded. The people in the village became very rich. The Village Headman made it mandatory that everyone in the village knew swimming. This was to ensure people did not lose lives if they accidentally slipped and found themselves in strong currents.

One young man, popularly known as Kamiso, and his wife Nyadani, were among the skilled fish catchers in the village. Kamiso could swim through fast-flowing water and reach areas where fish was in abundance. Kamiso became very famous and rich. When they had raised enough money, Kamiso and his wife decided to move to the city to start a bigger business. A lot of people in the village wished them well, though they were sad to see them leave the village.

Kamiso and Nyadani were very kind and generous people. After setting up their business in the City, they invited the people in their village to stay with them whenever they visited the City. Because of the open invitation, Kamiso and Nyadani had visitors from the village almost every week. Kamiso's wife, Nyadani, made sure the visitors were taken care of very well while Kamiso managed the business. People from the village loved Kamiso and his wife. They also offered Kamiso and his wife their homes should Kamiso and Nyadani decide to visit the village.

Kamiso and his wife continued to make progress with their business and had children. Their children did not have an opportunity to learn the swimming and fish-catching skills like their parents as there was no river near the city. Their parents were also very busy with managing the business such that their focus was mainly on the education for their children and not swimming and catching fish.

After many years, Kamiso and Nyadani planned to take their children to the village. They decided to take a holiday during the time when the river flooded so their children could have an experience of what happened in the village when the river flooded, and for the children to also join in the fun of catching the fish.

Kamiso and Nyadani arrived at the village with their children in time for the floods. When they had rested, the people in the village invited Kamiso's children to participate in the catching of the fish. Kamiso cautioned his children against going near fast-flowing water as they neither had experience in catching the fish nor swimming. The children assured their parents that they would stay away from any danger.

The fish-catching activity was so exciting that the children forgot about their inability to swim. They joined their friends in scooping the fish from the fast-flowing water. Unfortunately, one of Kamiso's children slipped and fell into fast-flowing water. The friends tried to catch him before falling into the water but missed. He was taken by the fast-flowing water down-stream.

When the people saw what had happened, they immediately sounded the drums to alert the people down-stream. The use of drums was the traditional way of sending information to the villages down-stream alerting them of anything. The sounds and beating of the drums differed for different messages. Use of the drums was the quickest way of communicating with the villages down-stream. On hearing the drums, the villagers downstream would know what to expect. On this occasion they knew that someone had fallen into the water. They got ready to do their best to rescue the person.

Fortunate enough, Kamiso's child was rescued from the fast-flowing water though at this time he was unconscious. They did everything they knew to resuscitate the child who had drowned. Kamiso's child regained consciousness by the time his parents and the other villagers reached the village down-stream. Kamiso and other villagers were very grateful to the down-stream villagers and took the boy back to their village.

When they arrived back at the village, the adults in talking to both the Kamiso and his children, used the proverb: '*If you are wearing tattered skirt, do not dance near the fire'*. They were, however, all happy that the boy was rescued and that he was aware of the risks associated with fishing in the flooded river.

Kamiso and his family enjoyed their holidays and returned to the city without any other incident. Kamiso's children used the proverb on themselves whenever one of them seemed to be doing something that made them vulnerable, the would say: '*If you are wearing a tattered skirt, do not dance near the fire*'

Break the Gourd

ONLY A GIRL WHO DOES NOT DRAW/FETCH WATER
DOES NOT BREAK THE GOURD (CALABASH)

This proverb may be seen as stereotype by many people. However, long time ago in Zambian cultural set-up, drawing of water from either the river or the well, was mostly the task of the women and girls. In those early days, water was drawn from the rivers using gourds (Calabashes), which women carried on their heads. A gourd is a large round fruit with a hard skin, and often used to carry water. The gourd does become slippery when wet and can easily slip off the hands of a person carrying it. Being a form of plant, they easily break, resulting in the loss of the water. Most women and girls would break a few of them in their lifetime. It was, therefore, an expectation that a woman or a girl who frequently drew the water would eventually break a few. If any woman claimed not to have broken a gourd in her life, then most people would conclude that she never drew the water.

The proverb is used to explain that any person who claims not to have made errors in life could mean they never tried doing something. Elders would encourage the young people, who err, not to live blaming themselves the entire of their lives. Specifically, it was used to pacify the situation, and to encourage the affected young person that something could have gone wrong because he/she was trying to do the best. With this proverb in use, adults with erring children would not take the matter further. In modern English, it would be considered as 'a *good intention that has turned into tragedy'*.

To make children, and others, understand the meaning of this proverbs, many stories were told, one being this one:

Once a upon a time, when the earth was still in its virgin form, the Tortoise was very beautiful and his shell was round and very smooth, making other animals admire him. He would use his shell to entertain other animals. He would hide in his shell and make some maneuvers, which other animals could not do due to the risks of bruising themselves as they did not have a protective shell like that of the Tortoise. The Tortoise would make unique sounds when hiding himself inside and could sing as well. This made other animals desire to befriend the Tortoise, and to be around him most of the time.

Among the animals that desired to befriend the Tortoise was the Eagle. It did take long for the Eagle and the Tortoise to befriend each other, because the Tortoise also wanted to befriend the Eagle because of his ability to fly very high. Eagle would tell other animals of the beautiful sceneries he enjoyed when very high in the sky; something that the Tortoise desired to experience too.

One day, an opportunity arose for the Tortoise and the Eagle to chat with each other after the day's activities. The Tortoise asked the Eagle if he could also see the beautiful sceneries he saw when high up in the sky. The Tortoise's desire was enhanced further when the Eagle told the Tortoise the beautiful appearances of the areas below, and how he always found it hard to fly back to the ground leaving the beautiful sceneries. The Eagle also told the Tortoise that he could see where other animals lived and what they were doing. He gave an example of seeing the Lion failing to catch the Impala for its lunch. He said it was interesting to see the Lion yawning due to hunger after failing to find alternative food.

The Tortoise begged the Eagle to take him up in the sky so he could also experience what the Eagle talked about. The Eagle was not keen taking the Tortoise with him that high in the sky as he was not certain of how the Tortoise would behave when excited. The Tortoise however, assured the Eagle that he would follow all the instructions given to him. An agreement was reached, and the Eagle agreed to take the Tortoise with him into the sky to see how things appeared on the ground from there.

On the day agreed to take the Tortoise into the sky, the Eagle reminded the Tortoise to stay on the Eagle's back and to hold firmly onto his feathers. The Eagle also told Tortoise not to scream when excited as that could easily make it harder for the Eagle to communicate with him.

The Tortoise climbed on the back of the Eagle, and they took off. At the beginning, the Tortoise was very compliant, holding firmly onto the feathers and stayed calm. As the Eagle went higher and higher into the sky, the Tortoise started getting excited and screaming to the Eagle. He was telling the Eagle what he saw below them. He then began to point at some things below them, in so doing letting go of his hold on the Eagle's feathers. The Eagle reminded the Tortoise again of the need to keep holding to the feathers. The Tortoise only settled for a short time, he again got excited when he saw several other things below them. He saw the river and some the Hippos. The Tortoise then saw a large field of mushroom which aroused his appetite. He started shouting to the Eagle and pointing to the field of mushroom below them. Suddenly, the Tortoise lost the grip on the feathers and slipped off the back of the Eagle.

The Eagle tried to catch the Tortoise midair, but he was too heavy for his craws to hold and stop him from continuing with the fall. The Eagle tried everything he could to stop the Tortoise from falling and hitting the ground very hard. Unfortunately, the Eagle could not manage to prevent the Tortoise from hitting the ground. The Tortoise fell on a rock, cracking his shell into many pieces. The Tortoise was unconscious for many months before he was able to talk again.

Although the shell healed it remained with very big cracks and lines showing the pieces of the shell. The Tortoise could not walk properly or quickly as before. Other animals started to laugh at the Tortoise. The Tortoise responded to their mocking by letting them know that he had no regrets because he had an experience of going high up into the sky, something that other animals would probably not be able to enjoy in their lifetime. Many animals that were sympathetic to the Tortoise's experience, praised him for being brave and reminded themselves that only those who do not try doing something never experience hardships. To encourage the Tortoise, other animals used the proverb that, *'only the girl that does not fetch/draw water does not break the gourd'*.

Carry Maize on the Head

WHEN YOU CARRY MAIZE ON YOUR HEAD FOWLS BE-
COME YOUR FRIENDS

This proverb is usually used to warn young people who seem to have a lot of friends hanging around them whenever they have something to offer. Parents warn the young ones that 'maize' in life can be compared to wealth, good living standards or good morals. Some friends may just want to use their wealth or assets, but once they no longer have the assets or wealth, they will 'fly' away (disappear), like fowls after eating the maize being carried by someone on their head. Adults and parents usually warn the young people to be careful as some friends may just be aiming at getting enjoying what they have to offer and abandoning them thereafter.

The context of the proverb is associated with women who used to carry maize (corn) on their heads. Although the corn would be in a container, sometimes hungry fowls, would invade the women, eating the maize they were carrying in the containers on their heads. Once the fowls were satisfied or the women reached their destinations, and put the containers down, the fowls would fly away.

To explain the proverb to young people, adults used stories like the one below:

A long time ago, in a certain village called Chaziya, there lived a devout man. The man had a lovely family and was committed to his family and the community. He had four children, three girls and a boy. The boy was called Bonongwe, but most people called him Bono, in short. Being the only boy in the family, Bono was the focus of the parents, in that traditionally, he was expected to protect his sisters. As per cultural practices at the time, he was also expected to know the culture to be able to represent the family in matters relating to his sisters' marriage arrangements.

Bono grew up following the footsteps of his father. He was committed to ensuring that his family was never embarrassed by his actions. Due to his parents' strictness, he grew up without interacting with other boys as his parents feared the other boys could influence him into doing things that the family did not approve of. He was always reminded of the dangers he could face from people who could just aim at spoiling the best things in his life.

When Bono completed his education, he moved to a big City to look for employment. The parents made sure he was engaged to a girl of their choice before he left the village. They feared city life could easily overwhelm him and result in Bono not having a good family. Bono was happy with all that his parents did.

Bono got a very good job in the city. He also managed to get a good accommodation in a lucrative suburb. After settling down, he went back home to marry his fiancé. After the wedding he took his wife with him to the city. Bono and his wife lived very happily for several years. He was committed to his wife, daily he would return home from work without passing through other places. If he needed to do some shopping, he would first go home and collect his wife for assistance. Many of his workmates would sometime mock Bono for not going out with them.

Later, Bono's wife noticed her husband coming home late. While Bono would always phone his wife during lunch, this also became irregular, and eventually he stopped. His wife wondered what was happening to her husband. Whenever she tried to ask him, Bono would either give various excuses or get angry at her, accusing her of being unappreciative and wanting to control him. His wife reminded Bono that sometimes friends could ruin his career if he did not take care of himself. Bono ignored all that his wife reminded him of.

Bono had been wooed into acquiring a girlfriend by his friends. One day while going home from work, Bono met a girl who asked to see the magazine he was reading. The girl commented that the magazine looked like the one she liked reading. As they talked about the magazine, he started to ask her many questions, which the girl did not manage to answer before reaching her drop-off point. As Bono found the conversation interesting and wanted to hear more, he dropped off the bus before reaching his usual drop-off point in order to continue talking to the girl. The girl's home was near the Bus stop and she invited Bono to her home to finish the conversation. By the time they concluded their conversation, it was very dark and raining. The girl invited Bono to have dinner with her and they continued talking while waiting for the rain to stop. Eventually, the conversation ended up somewhere where Bono could not resist the invitation to spend the night at the girl's place. Since then, their relationship became strong, and Bono started behaving strangely towards his wife.

The girl that Bono was dating was not married and was also not working. She found out that Bono had a very good job and was very caring. The girl resolved to get as much from Bono as she could before being abandoned by him, as was the case in the past when other men abandoned her after going out with her for a while. This time she resolved not to lose out again.

One day Bono went to his girlfriend's house for a casual visit. When he reached the house, the girl welcomed him and gave him food and a drink. Bono had forgotten that he had hinted on leaving her as he was having problems with his wife, who he did not want to lose. The girl had resolved not to let Bono leave her before she got what she wanted from him. She purposed to make Bono spend the whole week at her place on his next visit, Bono did not know that this casual visit was going to result in him spending the whole week at the girl's place.

Bono had gone to his girlfriend's house on a Sunday afternoon, and was planning on returning to his home to prepare for work the following day. However, after eating and drinking the drink she served him, he fell asleep. The girl had given him a strong alcoholic drink. Bono had never been exposed to strong drinks since he was born; the drink knocked him out. While he slept, the girl took all his clothes, including his under wear, washed and hanged them on the line some distance away from her house. The aim was to make sure Bono did not easily retrieve them if he wanted to return to his house earlier than she had wanted him to stay. The girl hanged the clothes on the line even though it was raining heavily.

Bono woke up in the early hours of the morning. He realized that he was not back at his house. He wanted to dress and leave so he could go home and prepare for work, but his clothes were no-where to be seen. He asked his girlfriend the whereabout of his clothes. The girl replied gently, telling him the clothes had been washed and were hanging on the line outside. Bono had no other clothes to use and could not fit into any of his girlfriend's clothes as she was very slim and shorter than him. Bono's only alternative was to stay on. The rain did not stop the whole day resulting in his clothes not drying.

Bono could not leave the house as he had no clothes, and he could not call his wife as his phone had also lost power. The girlfriend told him to relax and enjoy his stay with her. She was neither prepared to go out in the rain to get the clothes from the line nor go to shops to buy him anything. The girl made sure Bono understood that he was under her control. This went on for the whole week resulting in Bono not reporting for work. All his major assignments that he needed to complete that week were not done. Many clients were left disappointed, and others cancelled the contracts that they had with Bono's employers. His workmates, and the immediate Supervisor, did not understand what had happened to Bono for him not to report for work.

Rumour spread alleging that Bono had abandoned his work to be with his girlfriend. Bono's Supervisor followed through the leads from the rumours and found where he was. When Bono realised that the person knocking on the door was his immediate Supervisor, he told him that he could not come out of the house or allow him in as he did not have clothes on him. The Supervisor thought that Bono was just being arrogant and rude. He went back and summarily dismissed Bono.

When Bono finally managed to get back to his home, he found that his wife had also left the house together with all the children and household items. He had nowhere to go resulting in him becoming a destitute. He tried to go back to his girlfriend, but before he could reach the house, he saw another man entering the house and being hugged passionately by the girl. Bono could not do anything than walking away to find shelter at the refuge center.

The people who saw him started to talk among themselves. The wise man reminded everyone the proverb that said: '*When you carry maize on your head, fowls become your friends*'.

The Weather

This proverb is usually used to encourage people facing difficulties or challenges in life. The young people are urged to persevere in the face of difficulties. It also calls for bravery in the face of threats, and for the person to face the threats head on. The young people are also reminded that although some situations can never be reversed, adopting appropriate strategies could help deal with those situations in life. The weather in this proverb, is anything that life brings to anyone; can be good or bad. So, people are expected to get tough and face the challenges head on.

To explain this proverb and to make others remember it, adults told stories like the one below:

Once upon a time there was a man, known as Delepano, who was very good at herbal medicine. He was able to cure almost any type of disease. However, with time he became a Witch himself. His knowledge of the herbal medicine was so wide that he was feared by almost everyone in the village and the surrounding communities. Despite his good knowledge of the herbal medicine, he only had one child, a girl.

The girl grew up and reached the marrying age. Like anyone else, she was hoping to get married. Unfortunately, the girl could not get any young man approach her for marriage because everybody was afraid of her father. The families of any young man who heard that their son was seen near the girl would descend on the young man and threaten him of being disowned if he got involved with the daughter of the Witch. The girl could not find anyone to marry her.

After waiting and trying to get married for a long time, she decided to go to a distant country. When she arrived in that country, she undertook some studies. When she graduated, she managed to get a very good job. With time, she was able to find a very handsome man who wanted to marry her. The girl did not waste any time in accepting the man's proposal. Marriage arrangements were quickly finalised, and the wedding took place even though the man did not know much about the girl and her background. The girl also did not disclose much about her family fearing the would-be husband could walk away from her on hearing about her father being the Witch.

The couple lived together in their marriage for a long time, and they had their own children. After a while, the husband proposed to go and see his in-laws in his wife's village. The girl did not object to the suggestion, and went to the village with their children. Delepano was excited to see his daughter, grandchildren, and his only son-in-law. Delepano organised a very big feast to welcome his daughter and her family. Unfortunately, only a handful of people turned up for the function, something that made his son-in-law to wonder. After few days of being in the village, the son-in-law came to know the history of his wife's father.

Although the son-in-law would have wanted to divorce his wife, he was afraid of his father-in-law and how he could react on hearing his plans to divorce his daughter. He decided to wait until he went back to his family to seek guidance. His stay in the village was a miserable one due to the scary stories he heard about his father-in-law's witchcraft activities. He was so scared that he did not sleep most of the nights. He wished he could make the days run faster than they did.

The time of his stay in the village finally came to an end, and it was time to say farewell to his father-in-law. His father-in-law prepared a gift for him. The gift included a parcel, which his father-in-law told him to keep safely. He warned his son-in-law that losing the parcel or discarding it would spell doom on him and his family. He could not refuse to accept the parcel as he was already scared and worried for his own life.

When he arrived back to the city, he invited some of his family members and told them of all that he had seen and heard about his father-in-law. He also told them of the parcel that he was not to discard and how fearful he was about losing it. His family members asked what his intentions were. He told them that he wanted to divorce his wife and go somewhere without telling his wife and the children. This did not please the family members who did not want to see their relative become a destitute in another city, and his children living like orphans and suffering.

The family members asked him whether his wife had caused him any problems, and whether his wife practiced any witchcraft while at home. He told them that he had no problems with his wife, and that she did not practice or talk about witchcraft. The family members then rejected his reason for wanting to divorce her and leaving the children live as though they were orphans. They told him that they could have supported his decision to divorce had his wife been unfaithful or was engaging in witchcraft activities. They further said that her father's witchcraft activities were outside their home. They assured him that his father-in-law may have given him the parcel, the gift, to keep him and his family safe. They were certain that had the father-in-law intended to harm him, he could have done so while he was still in the village. They suggested that he remain committed to his wife and the children as the only way to avoid his father-in-law wanting to do anything bad to him and his extended family.

After some discussions, the elders and other family members told the man that divorcing his wife because of what he had heard about his father-in-law, was not morally and culturally right. They concluded by using the proverb: '*Once the millet has sprouted, it is not afraid of the weather*'.

What the Goats Say

THE LEOPARD DOES NOT SPEND SLEEPLESS NIGHTS
BECAUSE OF WHAT THE GOATS SAY

The proverb is used to urge the young people to focus on what they want to achieve in life, and not to be discouraged by degrading remarks from others. They are encouraged to consider their abilities, strengths and not weaknesses. The proverb emphasizes the importance of knowing that some talks are only meant to discourage them or cause emotional distress. It aims at assisting young people to only avoid the people or things that could truly harm them physically and/or emotionally. Further, the proverb encourages the young people to distinguish falsehood from reality, and to remind themselves that most talks are only meant to increase their vulnerability.

To illustrate the proverb, adults would tell stories like the one below:

A long time ago when animal population was far much greater than that of humans, and many modern gadgets and weapons had not yet been invented, there was a very big Kingdom called Kapatamoyo. The Kingdom had problems with the Lions, which seemed to have outnumbered other animals in the area by far, and the people were being targeted. Although the Kingdom had a lot of very skilled hunters, the Lions continued to terrorize the villages. To reduce the risk of people being killed by the Lions, the King mandated the elders in his Kingdom to train young men in better hunting skills.

Although the Kingdom had well-trained and skillful men in hunting, the problem of the Lions terrorizing them and attacking their livestock increased. This compelled the King to seek counsel of his elders to find a solution quickly. The elders advised the King that the only way to reduce the population of Lions in the Kingdom was to force young men to kill a Lion each. How that was to be implemented and achieved remained a big question. After deliberations, it was agreed that the only way to enforce the directive was to make it mandatory for any young man to kill a Lion and show his bravery before being allowed to marry the girl of his choice. The resolution was welcomed by all the King's counselors, and it was passed into Law. The Law which was passed and implemented to assist with cropping of the Lions in the Kingdom was also welcomed by every family. Those families with boy-child worked very hard to ensure their boys learnt better hunting skills and did not fail to marry when their time to marry came.

In that Kingdom, there was a young man called Dongosolo, who was popularly known as Dongo. Unlike all other young men of his age, Dongo did not have hunting skills because he refused to go hunting or learn how to hunt since he became of hunting-age. Other young men in the village talked badly about Dongo and mocked him each time they saw him. Dongo did not have friends among his peers because of their verbal attacks on his personality. His parents became worried each year that passed as they wondered how their son was going to prove his bravery at the time of marrying. Although the parents talked to Dongosolo about the matter, he did not seem to worry and did not argue with his parents. He assured them that when the time came, he would do whatever was required of him to marry. Despite these assurances, his parents remained concerned.

Dongosolo was a very fast runner. He could run faster than the Gazelles and could jump like an Impala. His ducking skills could not be compared to anyone in the Kingdom. However, his parents and other people in the Kingdom did not know this. Dongo would quietly sneak into the bush to practice running and jumping alone. After many years Dongo reached the marrying age, he approached his parents to assist him prepare for the marriage as per cultural practices. The parents reminded him of the requirement to kill a Lion to demonstrate bravery before he could be allowed to marry. Dongosolo politely responded by reminding his parents of the recent event they had all attended, where a young man failed to prove his bravery and was not allowed to marry. The response was enough to persuade his parents that he knew what was expected of him.

The parents organized a Spear, which was the only weapon available at the time, and a Lion's skin for Dongo to wear when going hunting. These were given to Dongo. However, Dongo had his own costume for the day that he had made for himself. The costume consisted long slips of rug-pieces which he was to wear around his waist and shoulders. He knew that while running they would be flying in all directions. He however, hid the costume from his parents fearing they would query him and possibly withdraw it from him. The parents were also expected to take a Goat to the King, as per tradition, for him to arrange a date for the Lion-killing event and to invite the people of the Kingdom.

The day of the event came for Dongo to demonstrate his bravery. His parents were not only worried about their son's lack of hunting skills but also feared he would be killed by the Lion. They were sweating profusely when the King emerged from his Palace and called the name of their son to go forward. Dongo went forward wearing the Lion's skin and a spear in his hand. Dongo had nicely folded his costume and could not be seen as he had it under the Lion's skin which he wore.

After all the traditional talks and rituals, Dongo left the people and went into the bush to find a Lion. He walked a long distance without seeing or meeting any. Just as he was wondering whether or not the Lions were there, he saw one a short distance from him. Dongo quickly untied his costume and the rugs hung over his shoulders and down from his waist. The Lion charged at him. Dongo started to run away from the Lion with his rugs flying all over him. With his speed, he increased the distance between himself and the Lion, which was getting irritated with the flying rugs on Dongo. He kept running until near the village when he slowed down. The Lion thought Dongo was tired, and it increased its speed to catch him. In front of Dongo there was a very big tree that had been pushed almost to the ground by the strong winds previous years and was leaning almost flat parallel to the ground with not enough space under it for anyone to pass through.

The Lion was almost reaching Dongo's flying rugs by the time Dongo reached the tree. The Lion could not see beyond Dongo and was distracted by the rugs when Dongo jumped over the tree just as the Lion was about to catch one of the flying rugs. The Lion, which had not seen the tree, when Dongo jumped over it, crashed into it very hard and fell backwards. The Lion roared from pain and was bleeding profusely. The people in the village heard the Lion's roar and thought Dongo had been caught by the Lion. The Lion, which was dazed after hitting into the tree tried to stand up but the pain was too much and thought Dongo had a weapon on him. The Lion, while staggering, started to run away from him. This gave Dongo the courage and motivation to start chasing it. He shouted on top of his voice, which further scared the Lion. In its confusion, it started running away from Dongo in the direction of the village unknowingly.

The people suddenly saw a Lion running towards the village with Dongo behind chasing it. The sight of the Lion caused confusion in the village as adults started screaming and shouting to warn the children of the danger. The children ran in all directions with parents trying to grab them to take them into houses for safety. The Lion got more confused and scared with the shouting and screaming and just kept running instead of attacking anyone. Dongo was almost catching up with the Lion when it jumped into the nearby bush and ran away at a very fast speed. The King, who had been surrounded by his guards, saw all this. The King laughed so loudly that even his guards were shocked as they had never seen or heard him laugh the way he did.

When the confusion had died down and everyone was settled, the King stood up to address the people. Dongo's parents did not know what to expect as their son had not killed the Lion. The King took some time before finding his composure, as he kept laughing without stopping. The King told his people that he had never seen something like what he had just witnessed since his birth; a Lion running away from a human being. He wondered what kind of a young man Dongo was that he made the Lion run away from him. In view of what had happened, he did not think Dongo had failed to kill the Lion, only that the Lion managed to escape from him. As such, Dongo was going to be allowed to marry any girl of his choice in his Kingdom.

Dongo's parents were overjoyed and offered to provide all that was required for him to marry a girl of his choice. The news about Dongo chasing the Lion spread throughout the Kingdom, prompting many people want to see him. While people talked, others remembered that this was the young man allegedly said to have been without hunting skills. The people realized that Dongo's peers had wanted to destroy his reputation without understanding his abilities, skills and tactics in dealing with the marriage challenge.

The Elders in the Kingdom concluded the talks about Dongo's response to what the people said about him, by citing the proverb; *'A Leopard does not spend sleepless nights because of what the Goats say'*.

ABOUT THE AUTHOR

Danny Phiri was born in the Eastern part of Zambia. He is the fifth born in the family of nine siblings. He is married to Gertrude Phiri and have three children, two girls and one boy.

His passion to work with children started while he was still in High School. He was the Sunday School Teacher at his local

Church. It was the interest in working with young ones that motivated him to become a teacher. He got his first Degree as the Science Teacher, later studied for an Honors Degree in Community Development. He also attained a Social Work Degree while working with the then Department for Child Protection and Family Support in Southwest Region as the Group Home Manager and Team Leader. This role brought him into close interaction with vulnerable children in the Out of Home Care.

It was his engagement with disadvantaged communities that qualified him for the inaugural Ciara Glennon Scholarship in 2002. Through the Scholarship Danny received a master's degree in Leadership from the University of Notre Dame Australia (UNDA). While her death was, and remains tragic, Ciara's life has sprouted through many others that have received assistance through the scholarship, and are now serving in various sectors including Health, Defence, Education, Transport and Local Government: May Her Soul Rest in Eternal Perfect Peace.

Danny is one of the elders in the Zambian community in Australia. He has participated in numerous community activities over the past number of years. This led to him being awarded a Community Service recognition award by the organisation of Zambians Living in Western Australia in 2017.

Danny is also a founding member of the African Professionals of Australia (APA), an organisation whose aim is to support professionals of African origin, empowering them to reach their full potential in their chosen field.

Danny's story telling skills have been his strength, especially in engaging with various community members. It was his oratory skills that propelled him into becoming the Community Mobilization Specialist with the International HIV/AIDS Alliance in Zambia in 2004. He continues to use his oratory skills whenever an opportunity arises, both in his family and the community. It is only when you have come face to face with him that you recognize his unique ability to engage with people of all ages.

www.ingramcontent.com/pod-product-compliance
Lightning Source LLC
Chambersburg PA
CBHW060548100426
42742CB00013B/2494